BOTS & BOSSES

BOTS &
BOSSES

THE HILARIOUSLY CHAOTIC SYMPHONY OF
MANAGEMENT IN THE AGE OF AI

JOHN BINKS

Bots & Bosses: The Hilariously Chaotic Symphony of Management in the Age of AI

For more information, email John@Binks.net.
ISBN: 9798853026889

TABLE OF CONTENTS

FOREWORD

I was motivated to write this book due to my keen interest and expertise in the intersection of artificial intelligence and management. I recognized that AI is revolutionizing numerous industries, and management practices are no exception. However, there are a lot of misconceptions and fears about implementing AI in managerial roles, and I wanted to demystify this notion.

I aimed to provide a comprehensive yet accessible guide that helps managers understand how AI can enhance their work rather than threaten it. I wanted to illuminate how AI can automate routine tasks, help with data-driven decision-making, and even strengthen the personalization of employee management without erasing the human touch that is so integral to effective leadership.

Moreover, addressing the ethical considerations when implementing AI is crucial, as these discussions are often overlooked yet vitally important. I sought to instill a sense of responsibility in my readers, making them aware of their role in ensuring AI is used ethically and judiciously.

Finally, I wanted to approach this potentially intimidating topic with humor and relatability to engage a broad range of readers. Writing this book allowed me to use my knowledge to facilitate understanding, promote ethical AI use, and, hopefully, contribute to AI's practical and positive implementation in management.

INTRODUCTION

Welcome, dear fellow Homo sapiens, to the cosmic dance of management in the brave new world where artificial intelligence reigns supreme. Once upon a time, your biggest worry as a manager was motivating Larry from Accounting to stop dozing off during meetings. Now, it's deciphering the difference between your Siri's sarcasm and Alexa's passive-aggression!

In "Bots & Bosses," we'll laugh, cry, and possibly question the nature of our reality as we navigate the uncanny valley of managing in the age of AI. Remember, while AI might steal the show, it's the humans backstage who, indeed, run it!

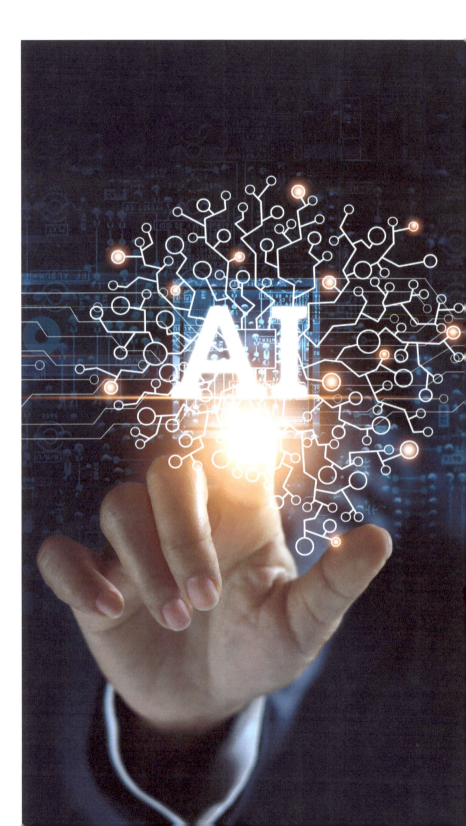

CHAPTER I

"HEY SIRI, HOW DO I MANAGE THIS TEAM?"

In the annals of human history, we never imagined a scenario where Siri, once a humble digital assistant consulted for the most trivial matters such as providing directions to the nearest sushi joint, would become an integral workforce member, offering innovative ideas on sushi-rolling techniques. In this opening chapter, we will deeply dive into the fascinating world of artificial intelligence in the workplace. Our exploration will lead us to understand how to manage this digital workforce without feeling threatened or, even worse, obsolete.

So, you've officially crossed the threshold into the brave new world of team management in the era of AI. It's an adventure akin to playing chess simultaneously with a toddler, who's just beginning to grasp the basics of the game, and a supercomputer, who knows every possible move. Don't panic! You certainly won't need a Ph.D. in Quantum Physics or a minor in Astrology to navigate these waters. Just prepare your favorite brew, find a comfy chair, sit back, and let's embark on this journey of discovery, unraveling the mysteries of AI in team management one laugh at a time.

AI team members are different from your typical human colleagues. Don't be startled if your AI teammate doesn't respond to your friendly office banter or chuckle at your jokes. It's not them; it's you. No, I'm just kidding. The reality is that AI, at this stage, doesn't comprehend humor or sarcasm unless explicitly programmed to do so, and even then, the attempts at humor can be as dry as a packet of silica gel you find in a new purse. AI is laser-focused, here for one thing and one thing only: to get tasks done. They work tirelessly, don't slack, and certainly don't care who has been crowned the champion of the latest season of "Dancing with the Stars."

Communication with AI has its own unique set of challenges. Have you ever experienced an embarrassing miscommunication because of your not-so-clear instructions to a human colleague? Brace yourself; it gets more intriguing with AI. If you thought human misunderstanding was hilarious, wait until you see an AI turning your vaguely worded command into an office disaster of epic proportions. To avoid this, it's crucial to ensure your instructions are as clear and detailed as the instructions you find on a shampoo bottle - simplicity and repetition are key.

Remember that emotional roller coaster ride you went on when Bob from Marketing nonchalantly took the last donut during team breakfast? Well, your AI colleague doesn't. It doesn't have feelings or emotional attachments. It doesn't care about donuts or Bob's insatiable appetite. Your AI team member is like Spock from Star Trek, entirely logical for a fault and emotionally unavailable. While the emotional ignorance of AI can sometimes serve as a refreshing break from office drama, remember that emotions fuel creativity and intuition and add that invaluable human touch that machines cannot replicate.

Your AI teammate will be someone other than the one to engage in friendly banter during coffee breaks. They're not going to contribute a homemade casserole to your office potlucks either (the silver lining? More food for you!). While you can't expect them to be the life of the office party, you can count on them to be the most reliable, hard-working team members who will never take your lunch from the fridge without asking.

The world of AI turns traditional notions of training and development on its head. Forget everything you know about conventional workforce development. With AI, no inspirational talks, no team-building exercises, and certainly no trust falls. Instead, their development involves software updates, algorithm tweaks, and some coding boot camps for you to understand their language and mechanisms better.

Finally, it's crucial to remember to use AI for what they are best at - performing repetitive tasks, carrying out complex data analysis, scheduling appointments, and so on. This strategic utilization will not only make your operations smoother, but it will also free up your human employees to focus on tasks requiring strategic thinking, decision-making, and creative problem-solving (and perhaps even a bit of time browsing social media – yes, I'm checking if you're still paying attention).

Ultimately, managing AI is not about extracting the maximum output from your new AI team member. It's about creating a harmonious symphony between the digital and the human, between cold logic and warm emotion, and between ruthless efficiency and out-of-the-box innovation. As the maestro of this unique orchestra, your baton will guide this amalgamation of man and machine. Your role as a team manager has never been more crucial or exciting. No pressure, though! Enjoy the ride and embrace the challenge as you enter this brave new world.

CHAPTER 2

"PRETEND TO BE HUMAN: THE AI IN YOUR TEAM."

Ah, the unparalleled joy of knowing that your latest team member won't ever request a vacation, a sick day, or even a coffee break. They'll never come in late after a night out or need a personal day to deal with a breakup. In this second chapter, we're going to dive headlong into the nuts and bolts (quite literally) of understanding AI. We will delve into their work ethics, quirks, strengths and limitations, and how you can tell when they're (metaphorically) laughing at your jokes.

You've managed to sail through Chapter 1, either because you found it riveting, informative, and perhaps even a bit entertaining or simply because you're the kind of person who never gives up quickly. Either way, I must confess, I'm genuinely thrilled to have you back! Now, let's continue our journey into the fascinating world of AI team members, unraveling the enigma they represent without turning it into a nerve-wracking, apocalyptic "Terminator" sequel.

Introducing an AI to your team is an experience that's far from your typical "meet and greet." They won't need a parking spot for their car (because they don't drive or need transportation), they won't lay claim to your favorite coffee mug (because they don't drink), and they certainly won't be belting out their favorite tunes during office karaoke (although, that could be a good thing). But what they will do, from the very first day, is be ready to work. They require no motivational pep talks, introductory orientation, ice-breaker exercises, or office tours. They're here to work, and they hit the ground running.

Unlike Joe from Accounting, who always has an elaborate coffee order each morning and never misses an opportunity to show off the adorable pictures of his cute dog, your AI team member won't have any personal quirks or pets to chat about. However, their uniqueness and individuality lie in their intricately designed algorithms, customization options, and powerful adaptive learning capabilities. If you were to think of AI as a car, you're both the driver, controlling its actions and the mechanic, fine-tuning its performance and making adjustments as you journey together.

Understanding AI is about something other than bonding over a pizza during lunch or discussing shared hobbies or interests. After all, their claim would likely revolve around data processing speeds and optimization algorithms, not precisely riveting lunchtime chat. Understanding AI is about learning its capabilities and limitations. AI is not a miracle worker (despite what some sci-fi movies might suggest). However, it can sometimes come exceptionally close, especially when handling colossal amounts of data in ways humans would find impossible.

Conversing with an AI team member won't involve sharing inspirational quotes or philosophical debates about life's meaning. AI prefers clear, precise instructions. Think of it as the world's most literal interpreter - it doesn't understand implications, hidden meanings or read between the lines. And no, despite what you might be hoping, it will only appreciate your office slang or in-jokes if specifically programmed to do so.

Providing AI feedback won't involve using soothing words or constructive criticism wrapped in layers of positive comments. AI works on data inputs and code adjustments. On the bright side, an AI team member won't take feedback personally, sulk in the corner, or hold a grudge. But remember, just like humans, they're not perfect and will require your patience (and a well-developed sense of humor) during the learning and adjustment process.

The gap between human and AI intelligence is real and undeniable. AI can work tirelessly, process information at incredible speeds, and stay unaffected by emotions, office politics, or personal problems. Yet, it won't understand the joy of finishing a complex project, the frustration of dealing with a difficult client, or the sheer hilarity of a well-timed pun. This gap, this divergence, makes us unique, human, and them, well, incredibly handy and efficient!

Understanding your AI team member is like figuring out a complex puzzle with no corners or edge pieces. It's challenging, bewildering, and can even be frustrating at times. But the gratification, the sense of achievement when things start to click into place and make sense, is unmatched. Keep laughing, learning, and exploring, and remember; the goal isn't to turn AI into humans but to create a team. This synergy can work together perfectly, complementing the other's strengths and overcoming their weaknesses.

CHAPTER 3
"THE BIG DATA DILEMMA"

The era of Big Data is akin to having an overly excited Labrador Retriever puppy in your hands - you adore the energy, the enthusiasm, and the boundless joy it exudes. Still, keeping up with its antics can be tiring and sometimes overwhelming. In this third chapter, we will guide you on training this data beast and harness its boundless energy and curiosity, channeling it into something that can be immensely beneficial for your organization.

As we begin this journey, I'd like to share a small joke to lighten the mood and break the ice: Why was the computer cold at the office? Because it left its Windows open! Hopefully, that brought a smile to your face. Now that we've giggled let's dive into this exciting and fascinating world, grins first.

If we had to personify AI, think of it as that one friend or acquaintance in your circle who somehow finds inexplicable joy in organizing their sock drawers by color, fabric, and perhaps even the day of the week. They relish tasks many of us would discover mundane, tedious, and utterly dull. Repetitive tasks that have the potential to turn our brains into mush - like data entry, sorting through hundreds of emails, processing countless transactions, or organizing mountains of data - are what AI considers its jam, its comfort zone.

In the world of AI, consider data as the equivalent of an all-you-can-eat buffet. An array of information and numbers, a feast that it can savor endlessly. They can chew through gigabytes of data, process it, analyze it, and draw insights from it quicker than you can say "spreadsheet." While humans are still figuring out how to split the restaurant bill evenly among five people, the AI has already calculated, processed, and drawn inferences from the GDP of a small country.

Unlike you, me, or any other human, AI doesn't need coffee breaks to recharge its energy, power naps to rest its consciousness, or a much-awaited annual vacation to refresh its spirit and enthusiasm. It can work round the clock, tirelessly, relentlessly, without so much as a yawn or a hint of fatigue. However, it is vital to ensure that while we harness this potential, we must not let it take over our role completely. After all, Skynet and the rise of the machines is pure fiction... right?

AI's have this uncanny ability to learn, adapt, and improve at a pace that leaves even the most ambitious and hard-working humans in the dust. They spot patterns, trends, and irregularities faster than a toddler spots a candy jar. However, unlike us, the upgrades and improvements in AI don't involve inspirational TED Talks, motivational seminars, or self-help books but rather involve tweaks in their algorithms and the addition of new datasets to their knowledge banks.

Regarding precision, AI could give a Swiss watchmaker or a German car manufacturer a run for its money. Their razor-sharp accuracy and attention to detail are lifesavers, especially in roles and scenarios that demand exactness and pinpoint precision. The bad news, unfortunately, is that AI, despite its incredible abilities, still can't predict lottery numbers. Trust me, I've tried.

For all its abilities, strengths, and advantages, AI does have its limitations. They can't brainstorm creative ideas, they can't empathize with a frustrated customer, they can't appreciate a beautiful sunset, and they certainly can't enjoy the excitement and camaraderie of Friday beers. These are the arenas where we, the humans, shine the brightest. So, fear not; AI is here to aid us, to make our lives easier, not usurp us.

In conclusion, getting the most out of your AI is about understanding its abilities, strengths, weaknesses, and limitations. It's not about making it replicate human abilities but using it to complement our strengths to aid us in tasks where we struggle. Remember, you're the captain on this journey, and AI is your trusty first officer. You set the course, the direction, and let's together explore this final frontier, this brave new world of endless possibilities.

CHAPTER 4

"ARTIFICIAL VS AUTHENTIC - THE BATTLE OF INTELLIGENCES"

What happens when your AI outperforms your star employee or, worse, your entire human workforce? The question isn't "if" but "when." It's a certainty we must face as we push further into artificial intelligence. So, buckle up and join me as we dive headfirst into a comprehensive, fun-to-read guide to managing the imminent IQ clash. Our objective is to navigate this delicate dynamic without sparking a human vs. robot rebellion or creating an atmosphere of resentment and fear.

An AI is as similar to a human team member as an apple is to an orange, or perhaps even more fittingly, an apple to a solar-powered toaster. While they all have unique qualities and uses, comparing them directly or expecting the same things from them is like expecting a fish to climb a tree. Recognizing and acknowledging these differences, including distinct working styles, diverse strengths, and unique limitations, is the first step in harmonizing the working relationship between these two very different entities.

Your AI must understand sarcasm, decipher vague instructions, and certainly won't appreciate your witty banter or the nuances of office humor. It won't perceive subtleties or read between the lines. It thrives on clear, concise, and precise communication. That's the language AI understands best, and learning to speak it fluently and efficiently can make all the difference in how effectively you can utilize it.

Remember, AI loves monotony, routine, and the predictable, while humans thrive on variety, novelty, and spontaneity. AI finds joy in tasks that humans often consider tedious, repetitive, or dull. Assigning roles and responsibilities based on this fundamental difference can enhance productivity and efficiency while keeping everyone (and everything) in the team happy, motivated, and engaged. It's a simple yet effective strategy of playing to everyone's strengths.

Feedback, criticism, and suggestions for improvement for humans often involve a delicate balance of constructive criticism, motivation, positive reinforcement, and a little handholding. For AI, it's an entirely different ball game. It's all about data, updates, and algorithms. No feelings will be hurt; no egos will be bruised. It's about identifying errors or inefficiencies and making the objective, emotionless tweaks and adjustments. Implementing a robust feedback mechanism for both, respecting their unique needs and requirements, can ensure a smooth running, continuously improving, and harmonious team.

Just as humans need training, mentoring, and education to upskill and improve, AI requires regular updates to improve its performance. It might not need inspirational seminars or team-building activities, but it thrives on new data, updated algorithms, and continuous learning. Its growth and evolution are as necessary and vital as its human counterparts, albeit in a very different way.

Harmonizing AI and human teams is about more than just turning humans into robots or vice versa. It's not about replacement but about enhancement. It's about creating a symbiotic, balanced relationship where both entities can do what they do best. It's about creating a diverse team of unique talents, where each member contributes something irreplaceable, leading to a balanced, productive, and harmonious workplace.

Remember this: AI might be the shiny new toy in the corporate world, the new kid on the block capturing everyone's imagination. But it's still just a tool, a means to an end. You, the human, are the one in charge, the leader, the visionary driving the team towards success. So, here's to you, the maestros conducting the symphony of human and AI harmony! May this fascinating music play on, creating a symphony that resonates with progress, harmony, and success.

CHAPTER 5

"DON'T TAKE IT PERSONALLY – IT'S JUST AN ALGORITHM"

It's a universally acknowledged truth in our digitized world that an AI with rapidly evolving abilities must require a proficient manager. The management of AI is an art and science, as these complex entities, while seemingly devoid of feelings, can sometimes display obstinacy and inflexibility that may remind one of a stubborn toddler. This chapter will arm you with the knowledge, insights, and techniques needed to 'communicate' effectively with these oh-so-logical and often inscrutable algorithms.

Before we tackle this somewhat daunting topic, let's lighten the mood a bit. Here's a chuckler: Why don't computers take their coffee with sugar? Because it makes them crash! Now, with your funny bone duly tickled, let's dive into the often-dreaded, occasionally frustrating, but always intriguing topic of AI mishaps.

Just like a toddler taking their first tentative steps or a newly promoted intern trying to navigate their new responsibilities, AI is bound to stumble, trip, and occasionally fall flat on its metaphorical face. AI errors can manifest in many ways - from misinterpreting data, sending emails to the wrong client, and drawing erroneous conclusions that could impact your decision-making process. Understanding and accepting that errors are inherent in the AI growth process can make handling these inevitable bumps in the road less of a hair-pulling, stress-inducing affair.

It's crucial to remember that AI isn't some all-knowing oracle, a magic crystal ball that flawlessly predicts outcomes or makes perfect decisions every single time. It's a tool that reflects the data and instructions fed into it. Mistakes often stem from something other than the AI but from erroneous inputs, incomplete or misleading data, or ill-defined algorithms. So, resist the urge to blame the messenger or to take these errors personally!

When an AI blunder occurs, it's time to don your Sherlock Holmes hat, pull out your magnifying glass and get down to some serious detective work. Is the problem with the data you've provided? Is there a flaw or bug in the algorithm? Do the instructions need to be more precise, specific, or accurate? Finding the source of the error can often feel like solving a complex murder mystery sans the dramatic background music, slow-motion scenes, and moody, noir lighting.

Early detection, regular monitoring, and swift correction are crucial to managing AI errors. Regular check-ins, reviews, and audits can help spot anomalies, glitches, and mistakes before they snowball into full-blown disasters. Remember, an ounce of prevention is worth a pound of cure, or in our case, countless hours of damage control, lost productivity, and red-faced apologies.

Post error, it's time to roll up your sleeves, dust off your teaching hat, and get back to training your AI. Incorporate the lessons learned from the error, update the data, clarify the instructions, tweak the algorithm, or adjust the parameters as needed. Yes, it's like repeating a school grade without the awkward puberty phase, schoolyard bullies, and pop quizzes.

Every AI error is an opportunity for learning, growth, and improvement, both for the AI and for you, its human trainer and manager. Embrace these hiccups, stumbles, and missteps as steppingstones toward a more effective, efficient, and reliable AI. Remember, even diamonds, those stunning gems of breathtaking beauty and remarkable strength, need a little pressure, time, and polishing to shine truly!

To wrap up, managing AI errors is less about panicking, stressing out, or throwing your hands up in defeat and more about patience, calm analysis, swift action, and, yes, a dash of humor to lighten the mood. So, the next time your AI sends out a company-wide memo in binary, books a flight to Mars for the annual meeting or decides that everyone should take a coffee break at 3 AM, take a deep breath, smile, and dive into problem-solving mode. After all, a little chaos, a few unexpected detours, and the occasional bump in the road make the success story all the more exciting and the journey all the more memorable!

CHAPTER 6

"AUTOMATING OFFICE POLITICS – A CAUTIONARY TALE"

Indeed, AI technology advancements are revolutionizing how we work, transforming our workflows, enhancing productivity, and ushering us into a new era of digital innovation. Yet, there's one element of the traditional workspace that AI is yet to master, perhaps thankfully so, the intricate, nuanced, and often perplexing art of office politics. In this part of our journey, we'll delve into the fascinating challenge of managing the delicate balance between human and AI colleagues, preventing potential faux pas, and maintaining a harmonious, productive, and inclusive work environment.

The linchpin of a successful, efficient, and vibrant workplace in this brave new world is the harmonious coexistence of AI and human employees. Think of it as an odd couple sitcom, a buddy comedy, where two very different beings with unique strengths, quirks, and capabilities learn to live and work together. They navigate misunderstandings, tackle challenges, celebrate victories, and adapt to each other's quirks, providing us with laughs, memorable moments, valuable insights, and hopefully handsome profits.

In the evolving world of AI, there are no stupid questions, irrelevant concerns, or insignificant doubts. Foster an atmosphere of curiosity and encourage open, honest communication about AI—its purpose, its functionality, how it operates, and the changes it brings to the team and the organization. This ensures everyone is on the same page, or at least reading from the same book, minimizing confusion, miscommunication, and resistance to this digital shift.

A team that works together collaborates effectively, respects each other's contributions, and understands each other's roles, thrives together, even when that team is a blend of humans and AI. Foster a supportive environment where AI is viewed not as a threat, faceless, emotionless replacement but a collaborator, a teammate, and a tool to enhance productivity and efficiency. After all, having a friendly, reliable robot co-worker can be a great conversation starter and an intriguing glimpse into our technologically advanced future!

With AI taking over routine, mundane tasks, humans can upskill, expand their horizons, and take on more complex, creative, and intellectually stimulating roles. Support this transition with adequate training programs, continuous learning opportunities, and ample resources. Remember, while an AI might be able to calculate faster, churn out reports quicker, or analyze data more efficiently, it can't replicate human creativity, critical thinking, or intuition.

Build trust in AI by being transparent, open, and upfront about its usage, capabilities, limitations, and role in the organization. Also, ensure that your AI adheres to ethical standards, upholding the same principles of fairness, integrity, and respect as its human counterparts. It should be included in the ethical considerations and company values because it can't join the office party, share anecdotes by the water cooler, or participate in the annual talent show.

Celebrating successes, lauding achievements, and acknowledging milestones, whether achieved by humans or AI, helps foster a positive, inclusive, and uplifting culture. So, the next time your AI system reaches a significant milestone, remember to recognize its success. You might need help to give it a high five, treat it to a celebratory dinner, or present it with a shiny trophy. Still, a well-earned system upgrade, a software update, or an expansion of its capabilities can be a fitting pat on the back!

In conclusion, fostering a healthy, robust, and harmonious AI-infused culture is about acceptance, collaboration, transparency, mutual respect, and constant growth. It's about reminding everyone (and every AI) that they're valuable, appreciated, and integral team members. It's about integrating this digital shift seamlessly into the fabric of your organization, creating a hybrid workplace that's future-ready, dynamic, and stimulating. So, here's to the new era of water cooler moments—may they be full of binary jokes, amusing glitches, surprising breakthroughs, and laughter that's as infectious as genuine!

CHAPTER 7

"AI IN PERFORMANCE APPRAISALS - A NEW ERA OF OBJECTIVITY"

Performance reviews, a time-honored tradition in workplaces worldwide, are undergoing a radical transformation thanks to AI. Say goodbye to the days of pandering to Peter's overly sensitive ego or navigating through the stormy seas of Nancy's relentless negativity - get ready to embrace unbiased, straightforward, objective, and data-driven assessments. And for those who've been banking on their exceptional golfing skills or a knack for telling hilarious jokes to sway the scales in their favor, here's a spoiler: AI doesn't care about your weekend hobbies or charisma. It's all about your performance, productivity, and contributions.

Before we embark on our enlightening exploration of AI ethics, here's a chuckler to lighten the mood: Why don't machines need to drive to work? Because they prefer to byte and teleport! Now that we've got our daily dose of humor and started the conversation on a light note let's tread the slightly more complex, challenging, and consequential path of AI ethics, a topic that's as compelling as it's vital.

With the advent of AI, we have immense, unprecedented power at our fingertips. But, as our favorite web-slinging superhero famously reminds us, with great power comes great responsibility. Our decisions about AI deployment, usage, and regulation have profound ethical implications that must be carefully considered, diligently addressed, and responsibly managed.

AI, in many ways, functions much like a mirror, accurately reflecting the biases, prejudices, and disparities present in its training data. If left unchecked, these biases could inadvertently perpetuate harmful stereotypes, reinforce discriminatory practices, and cause unjust outcomes. Acknowledging these inherent biases, actively working to minimize them, and continuously monitoring and rectifying any unintentional biases is a critical responsibility of every AI manager.

Privacy becomes a significant, pressing concern in an age where AI can swiftly process, analyze, and draw insights from vast amounts of data. Striking the right balance between leveraging data to enhance efficiency and respecting the privacy rights of individuals is like tightrope walking – it requires focus, balance, careful steps, and a sturdy safety net of solid privacy policies and strict data protection measures.

A black box AI, much like a secretive, rebellious teenager, can be a cause for worry, suspicion, and mistrust. Ensuring transparency in how AI makes decisions, learns and evolves, and operates helps build trust, allows for better error correction, and fosters accountability. It's about knowing the 'why' behind the 'what,' the reasoning behind the results, and the logic behind the learning.

When used thoughtfully, ethically, and inclusively, AI can significantly impact society. It can revolutionize sectors, from improving healthcare outcomes to enhancing education methodologies, from optimizing resource utilization to predicting and mitigating risks. However, ensuring these advancements don't inadvertently widen social inequalities, exacerbate digital divides, or cause unintended harm is crucial.

Given AI's far-reaching implications, potential risks, and transformative power, robust policies and comprehensive regulations are necessary to guide its use, ensure ethical compliance, and prevent misuse. This is less about hampering innovation or stifling creativity and more about providing a fair, safe, inclusive, and ethical AI landscape.

In conclusion, navigating the fascinating, complex maze of AI ethics isn't a one-time event but a continuous, evolving journey. It's about making informed, considerate decisions, learning from missteps and course corrections, and balancing innovation and ethics. It's about leveraging AI to drive profits and enhance efficiency, improve lives, advance societal progress, and promote fairness and equity. So, here's to using AI power responsibly - because we're not just managers, we're ethical superheroes, stewards of a brave new world powered by the synergistic fusion of technology and humanity!

CHAPTER 8

"THE FUTURE - HUMANOID BOSSES, ROBOT UNDERLINGS, AND WHAT'S IN BETWEEN"

In this chapter, we'll take a thrilling journey into the future. In this world, humanoid robots walk our office corridors, digital assistants lead our meetings, and artificial intelligence infuses our daily operations. Imagine a futuristic workspace where bots, algorithms, and humans work side by side, each contributing their unique abilities to achieve shared goals. As a manager, how will you adapt to this brave new world? How will you evolve, innovate, and lead in an era dominated by AI-driven management?

Before we embark on this exciting, enlightening, and possibly daunting journey, here's a playful riddle to kick-start our explorations: What do you call a computer that sings? A-Dell! Having shared a light-hearted moment, let's now strap on our virtual reality glasses, hop onto our hoverboards, and explore the uncharted territories of the future of AI-driven management.

Bid farewell to the days of forgetting important dates, scrambling for meeting notes, or feeling overwhelmed with the avalanche of emails. With AI personal assistants, every manager can have digital Jeeves in their pocket, making them more efficient, organized, responsive, and proactive. AI can assist you with your administrative tasks and enhance your decision-making abilities, making you a little less reliant on caffeine and a lot more reliant on data and insights.

As AI technologies advance, they become increasingly adept at pattern recognition, predictive analysis, and accurate forecasts. Your AI can be a reliable advisor, helping you make informed, data-driven decisions. At the same time, you focus on the big-picture strategy, human relationships, and leadership roles that require the unique capabilities only humans possess.

AI's ability to process vast amounts of data in real time and churn out precise insights makes it an invaluable tool for problem-solving. It's like having a super-smart, extremely diligent, tireless intern who's always ready to crunch numbers, analyze trends, and churn out solutions, all while you're asleep.

From designing personalized learning paths based on each employee's unique needs and goals to developing targeted wellness programs that boost employee health and well-being, AI can revolutionize how you manage the employee experience. AI can help promote engagement, increase productivity, and enhance job satisfaction by customizing and personalizing employee engagement, development, and wellness initiatives. With AI as your strategic partner, you might have your secret weapon to finally win that coveted "Best Place to Work" award.

Beyond business operations, AI can play a significant role in advancing sustainability efforts. From optimizing energy use to predicting climate trends, from enhancing resource utilization to driving sustainability initiatives, AI can be an ally in your mission to increase profits and positively impact the planet.

With AI technologies evolving at a dizzying pace, staying abreast of the latest developments, innovations, and advancements is crucial. Consider it a professional version of keeping up with the latest TV shows - but with more learning opportunities, fewer spoilers, and more potential to transform your career.

To wrap up, the future of AI-driven management is brimming with exciting possibilities, transformative potential, and opportunities for innovation. By embracing these advancements, learning to use them effectively, and integrating them strategically into our managerial styles, we can create an efficient, data-driven, and human-centered management ethos. So, buckle up, my fellow managers. The future is here, and it looks promising and AI-mazing! As we venture into this AI-infused future, let us strive to leverage AI not just as a tool but as a partner in our quest to create workplaces that are productive, inclusive, innovative, and humane.

CHAPTER 9

"AI MANAGEMENT MYTHS: BUSTING THEM WITH STYLE AND A SMILE"

Why did the scarecrow install AI in his field? Because he wanted outstanding performance in his field! A little humor goes a long way in setting a relaxed tone as we prepare to dive headfirst into an area filled with misconceptions and misunderstandings. That's right; it's time to unravel the tangled skein of AI management myths. These misconceptions have long plagued the conversations around AI in the workplace, sowing seeds of doubt and mistrust. In this chapter, we'll methodically address these myths and debunk them, shedding light on the reality of AI in the management sphere.

One of the most pervasive and deeply ingrained myths is the fear that AI will replace us, rendering human workers obsolete. As a manager, your role involves strategic thinking, emotional intelligence, decision-making, relationship-building, and leadership - elements that AI cannot replicate or replace in its current form and foreseeable future. It's important to understand that AI is not some omniscient, omnipotent entity bent on world domination. Instead, it is an incredibly potent tool, an aid designed to enhance human capabilities and efficiencies. So, breathe easy; your job is not on the AI hit list!

Another common misconception is that AI management is an esoteric realm, limited to those who speak fluent "geek," possess an intricate knowledge of programming, or have advanced degrees in computer science. This couldn't be further from the truth. With user-friendly interfaces, intuitive design, and a wealth of resources and learning tools, even the least tech-savvy manager can effectively command AI. Remember, you don't need to be an automotive engineer to drive a car. Similarly, you don't need to be a programmer or data scientist to leverage AI in your management strategies.

Many people erroneously believe that AI is an autonomous, self-managing entity like a perpetual motion machine. This, however, is different. AI systems require regular updates, checks, recalibrations, and, sometimes, course corrections. Just like you wouldn't water a houseplant once and expect it to flourish indefinitely, you can't "set and forget" an AI system. It needs consistent attention, adjustments, and maintenance to perform optimally and deliver the desired results.

A widespread myth that has triggered much anxiety and debate is the perception of AI as a "job stealer." However, the reality is that AI is designed to automate repetitive, mundane, and low-value tasks, freeing humans to focus on more complex, creative, and high-value aspects of their jobs. Thus, rather than stealing jobs, AI is more of a productivity booster, efficiency enhancer, and work-life balance facilitator.

Another myth that needs debunking is that AI can automate and replace the human touch. While AI can process data, generate insights, automate tasks, and even mimic specific human behaviors, it cannot replicate empathy, creativity, interpersonal relations, or emotional intelligence. These inherently human traits form the cornerstone of effective management and are far beyond the reach of even the most advanced AI. While AI may change how we work and manage, it doesn't take the 'human' out of 'human resources.'

In conclusion, understanding AI beyond the myths, misconceptions, and misunderstandings helps leverage its full potential and truly harness the power of this transformative technology. So, let's bid a firm farewell to these baseless misconceptions and embrace AI for what it truly is: a tool designed to help us be more effective, productive, innovative, and a little cooler. After all, not everyone can say they command a sophisticated, cutting-edge AI at work! The future of management is here, and it's not just automated; it's exciting, empowering, and AI-mazing!"

CHAPTER 10

"HITCHHIKER'S GUIDE TO AI IN VARIOUS INDUSTRIES"

In this grand finale, we won't leave you with a cliffhanger but with comforting reassurances and pragmatic strategies to navigate, survive, and thrive in this brave new world saturated with AI. We're stepping into an era where it's not just about mastering the CTRL+ALT+DEL sequence but about effectively employing AI tools across different industries to solve complex problems, enhance performance, and drive growth.

Healthcare is one of the industries that has seen dramatic changes with the integration of AI. AI is a digital doctor in this domain, analyzing vast amounts of data to diagnose diseases, recommend treatments, and even predict health risks. It's important to understand that the goal isn't replacing healthcare professionals but empowering them with a powerful tool to enhance patient care. Picture an assistant who can process thousands of patient records in a heartbeat, provide diagnosis suggestions based on the latest medical research, and accurately predict potential health risks. This is the potential of AI in healthcare, revolutionizing patient care and disease management without threatening the role of healthcare professionals.

Education is another sector where AI has made a significant impact. Here, AI has the potential to personalize learning paths, assess student progress in real time, and provide adaptive feedback. This application of AI is akin to having a dedicated tutor for each student but without the need for endless cups of tea or mountains of textbooks. It's about harnessing the power of AI to offer tailored, immersive, and engaging learning experiences to students, helping them learn at their own pace and in their style.

The financial industry has also welcomed AI with open arms. From detecting fraudulent transactions to providing insightful investment advice, AI has become the savviest financier. However, it's about more than making human finance professionals redundant but about supplementing their abilities with AI's precision, speed, and data-crunching capabilities. This synergy can turn a complex financial landscape into a pleasant stroll in the park.

Retail is another sector where AI is leading a revolution. From offering personalized shopping experiences based on consumer preferences and purchase history to intelligent inventory management and customer behavior analysis, AI is reshaping the shopping experience. It's like having a personal shopper who knows your preferences and budget and anticipates your whims and wishes.

In manufacturing, AI is making its mark through predictive maintenance, quality control, and optimization of production processes. Imagine a super-efficient engineer who works around the clock without breaks, doesn't grumble about overtime, and continuously strives to improve efficiency. That's what AI brings to the manufacturing industry, driving productivity and quality to new heights.

Entertainment is another industry being transformed by AI. It's shaping the way content is created, distributed, and consumed. Imagine a personal entertainer who knows your favorite genres, can recommend new content based on your preferences, and can even create original pieces tailored to your tastes. That's the power of AI in the entertainment industry, revolutionizing content creation and consumption.

In a nutshell, AI is a versatile traveler, hitching rides across different industries and bringing with it efficiency, personalization, innovation, and transformative potential. As managers and leaders, we must welcome this traveler, harness its potential, and guide its journey to ensure it contributes positively to our industry and society. We need to be the drivers who steer AI toward the destination of improved productivity, enhanced user experiences, and ethical practices. So, here's to the future of AI-powered industries – all packed, geared up, and ready for a thrilling ride on the highway of technological evolution!

EPILOGUE

"ADVENTURES IN AI-LAND: EMBRACING THE JOURNEY"

As we approach the conclusion of our journey, I have one last jest for you. What's a computer's favorite snack? Well, it's microchips, of course! We hope you've enjoyed our humor-filled, enlightening journey through AI-land just as much as our digital companions savor their bite-sized treats.

During this book, we have embarked on an adventurous exploration of the vast landscape of AI in management. Our journey has been lively, carefully treading the fine line between the informative and the entertaining. Together, we have explored the nooks and crannies of AI:

- The fundamental principles.
- The challenges come packaged with benefits.
- The ethical considerations that must be taken into account.
- The exciting potential that awaits us.

We have also thrown in some myth-busting for good measure, ensuring that our understanding of AI remains grounded in fact and not entangled by fiction.

So, what's the crux of the matter? What should we take away from this AI-saturated exploration? AI is a tool; like any tool, it's only as effective, transformative, and impactful as the person wielding it. It doesn't hold magical powers nor bring the doom of humanity, despite what dystopian science fiction might have you believe. As managers, leaders, and innovators, we have the opportunity – and perhaps the responsibility – to leverage AI's astounding capabilities to drive efficiency, enhance decision-making, foster creativity, and positively impact our teams, our organizations, and the world at large.

But let's be clear: the AI journey doesn't terminate here. As with any evolving technology, the march of progress never ceases. Our understanding and utilization of AI will continue to develop and refine itself, growing and changing as the technology matures. This calls for continuous learning, an openness to change, and a hearty sense of humor to make the journey enjoyable. These will serve as our guiding stars and compass as we navigate through the winding roads and vast vistas of this exhilarating AI frontier.

Here's an invitation to welcome AI into our management practices with open arms and an open mind, sprinkled with a few well-timed jokes for good measure. Let's raise a toast to an exciting future filled with the rhythm of binary code, the assistance of digital comrades, and, perhaps, the occasional AI blooper that reminds us of the endearing quirks of technological progress.

After all, being a manager in the age of artificial intelligence isn't solely about strategy, algorithms, and data - it's about the fascinating stories we will share, the discoveries we will make, and the tales we'll recount along the way. It's about the grand narrative we will weave, the saga of our collective experience in this AI-driven adventure.

Here's to us, to you, and to the journey that awaits us in the exciting world of AI. And remember, in the end, it's the adventure, the curiosity, and the shared laughs that will truly make this journey through AI-land unforgettable.

APPENDIX

RESOURCES AND TOOLS FOR BOT MANAGEMENT:

As managers in the age of AI, it is essential to understand the resources and tools available to effectively manage bots in the workplace. This appendix provides a comprehensive list of resources and tools that can help you navigate the chaotic symphony of management with bots and AI.

1. Bot Management Platforms:
   Bot management platforms are crucial for centralizing the management of your bots. These platforms provide features like monitoring, analytics, security, and deployment capabilities. Popular platforms include Botpress, Dialogflow, and IBM Watson Assistant. These tools will help you streamline bot development, deployment, and maintenance.

2. Natural Language Processing (NLP) Libraries:
   To enhance your bots' conversational abilities, NLP libraries are invaluable. Libraries such as NLTK, spaCy,

and Gensim provide pre-trained models and tools for text analysis, sentiment analysis, and named entity recognition. These resources enable your bots to understand and respond to user queries more effectively.

3. Bot Security Tools:
Ensuring the security of your bots is a top priority. Bot security tools like PerimeterX Bot Defender, DataDome, and Akamai Bot Manager can protect your bots from malicious activities, including bot attacks, scraping, and credential stuffing. These tools provide real-time threat intelligence, behavior analysis, and mitigation techniques to safeguard your bots and data.

4. Conversation Design Tools:
Creating engaging and user-friendly bot conversations requires specialized tools. Conversation design platforms such as Botmock, Botsociety, and Chatfuel allow you to design, prototype, and test bot conversations before deployment. These tools offer visual interfaces, collaborative features, and integrations with popular bot development platforms.

5. Bot Analytics:
To continuously improve your bots' performance, analytics tools play a vital role. Platforms like Botanalytics, Dashbot, and Chatbase provide in-depth metrics, user insights, and conversation logs. These tools help you measure user satisfaction, identify

bottlenecks, and optimize your bots' conversational flows.

6. Bot Maintenance and Monitoring:
   Keeping your bots running smoothly requires diligent maintenance and monitoring. Tools like Botpress Monitor, Botium, and BotManager offer features like error tracking, performance monitoring, and automated testing. These resources help you proactively identify issues and ensure optimal bot performance.

In conclusion, successfully managing bots in the modern workplace requires leveraging the right resources and tools. The appendix highlights various platforms and tools that can assist managers in developing, securing, analyzing, and maintaining bots. By utilizing these resources, you can navigate the chaotic symphony of management with bots and AI, ensuring a harmonious and productive relationship between bots and their bosses.

ACKNOWLEDGMENTS:

First off, a huge high-five to all the brave managers who've decided to join me on this rollercoaster of a journey. Your adventurous spirit in welcoming the mad world of AI into your workplaces has been the key to penning this epic tale. Without your flexibility to dodge the curveballs, "Bots & Bosses: The Hilariously Chaotic Symphony of Management in the Age of AI" would've been as exciting as a software manual.

Next, let's raise a virtual toast to the bots that have worked their circuits off in shaping this narrative. Your relentless efforts in making our lives easier (while secretly plotting world domination, I presume), have prodded me to dive headfirst into the enchanting whirlpool of AI and its intriguing influence on the modern work arena.

To my fellow AI enthusiasts and scholars, I doff my hat. Your groundbreaking revelations and your unyielding chase for wisdom have spiced up the ideas served in this book. It's through this camaraderie and mutual geeking out that we're steering through the labyrinth of AI-induced chaos.

And to my loyal cheering squad of family and friends, thank you for the constant pep talks and your unwavering belief in me. Your support has been the rocket fuel propelling me on this adventurous expedition.

So, here it is. "Bots & Bosses: The Hilariously Chaotic Symphony of Management in the Age of AI" wouldn't exist without this fantastic ensemble of managers, bots, fellow enthusiasts, and AI warriors. I sincerely hope this slightly eccentric guide serves as a trusty roadmap for managers and leaders trying to ride the AI wave and dance with the chaos it unfailingly brings. Together, we'll orchestrate the most melodious symphony of bots and bosses, tuning the future of work in the AI era.

www.ingramcontent.com/pod-product-compliance
Lightning Source LLC
Chambersburg PA
CBHW041146050326
40689CB00001B/499